# Diverse Divorce

## *Parenting through Separation*

# Table of Contents


1. Introduction ........................................................................... 1

2. Understanding the Journey of Separation ............................... 2

    2.1. Understanding Divorce ........................................................ 2

    2.2. Role of Communication ...................................................... 2

    2.3. Coping Strategies .............................................................. 3

    2.4. Co-Parenting ..................................................................... 3

    2.5. Building Resilience ............................................................ 4

    2.6. Final Thoughts ................................................................... 4

3. Priorities in Parenting through Change .................................. 5

    3.1. Change: Understanding and Navigating Through It ........... 5

    3.2. Recognizing the Needs of Your Child ................................. 6

    3.3. Healthy Coping Mechanisms ............................................. 6

    3.4. Co-Parenting Successfully ................................................. 7

    3.5. The Role of Self-Care in Parenting .................................... 7

4. Communicating Divorce to Children: Paths Less Travelled ..... 9

    4.1. Comfort Comes First ......................................................... 9

    4.2. Rehearse to De-Stress ....................................................... 9

    4.3. Simple, Straightforward, and Age-Appropriate Talk ........ 10

    4.4. The United Front .............................................................. 10

    4.5. Reassurance - The Power of Love ..................................... 10

    4.6. Addressing the Changes .................................................. 11

    4.7. Checking-In ..................................................................... 11

5. The Art of Co-Parenting Post-Separation .............................. 12

    5.1. Establishing Clear and Consistent Communication .......... 12

    5.2. Developing a Co-Parenting Plan ...................................... 12

    5.3. Fostering Emotional Stability for the Children ................. 13

    5.4. Creating and Maintaining Boundaries ............................. 13

    5.5. Cultivating Patience and Understanding .......................... 14

5.6. Emphasizing Teamwork and Flexibility . . . . . . . . . . 14

6. Navigating Child Emotions: Tears and Cheers . . . . . . . 15

6.1. Recognizing the Tears: Understanding Your Child's
Emotional Response to Divorce . . . . . . . . . . . . . . . 15

6.2. Addressing Anger and Frustration . . . . . . . . . . . 15

6.3. Managing Fear . . . . . . . . . . . . . . . . . . . . . 16

6.4. Dealing with Sadness and Grief . . . . . . . . . . . . 17

6.5. Tackling Guilt and Denial . . . . . . . . . . . . . . . 17

6.6. Cultivating the Cheers: Building Resilience and Positivity
Amidst Divorce . . . . . . . . . . . . . . . . . . . . . . . 17

6.7. Resilience-Building Games and Activities . . . . . . . 18

6.8. Coping Strategies . . . . . . . . . . . . . . . . . . . 18

6.9. Rebuilding Trust . . . . . . . . . . . . . . . . . . . . 18

7. Legal Landscapes: Children's Rights and Custody . . . . . 20

7.1. Understanding Children's Rights . . . . . . . . . . . . 20

7.2. Unravelling the Concept of Custody . . . . . . . . . . 21

7.3. Common Custody Arrangements . . . . . . . . . . . . . . 21

7.4. The Role of the Courts in Custody Decisions . . . . . . 22

7.5. Legal Representation for Children . . . . . . . . . . . 22

8. Alone, not Lonely: Redefining Solo Parenting . . . . . . . 24

8.1. Reigniting Your Personal Identity . . . . . . . . . . . 24

8.2. Building a Strong Support Network . . . . . . . . . . . 24

8.3. Strengthening Communication Channels . . . . . . . . . 25

8.4. Fine-tuning Parenting Strategies . . . . . . . . . . . 25

8.5. Nurturing Emotional Resilience . . . . . . . . . . . . 25

8.6. Quality Time and Unwavering Love . . . . . . . . . . . 26

8.7. Building Financial Stability . . . . . . . . . . . . . 26

9. Resilience: Thriving in the Face of Challenge . . . . . . 27

9.1. Understanding Resilience . . . . . . . . . . . . . . . 27

9.2. Building Resilience . . . . . . . . . . . . . . . . . . 27

9.3. Resilience and Separation . . . . . . . . . . . . . . . . . . . . . . . . . . . 28

9.4. A Model of Resilience . . . . . . . . . . . . . . . . . . . . . . . . . . . . . 29

9.5. Setting an Example . . . . . . . . . . . . . . . . . . . . . . . . . . . . . . 29

10. Healing Together: Empathetic Parent-Child approaches . . . . . . . 31

10.1. Navigating Conversations about Divorce . . . . . . . . . . . . . 31

10.2. The Art of Active Listening . . . . . . . . . . . . . . . . . . . . . . . 32

10.3. Sharing Feelings: Creating a Safe Space . . . . . . . . . . . . . . 32

10.4. Tools for Transition: Managing Change Together . . . . . . . . 33

10.5. Co-Parenting: The Power of Collaboration . . . . . . . . . . . . 33

11. Resilience in Action: Building Your Child's Strength . . . . . . . . . 35

12. New Beginnings: Building Life Post-Divorce . . . . . . . . . . . . . . 36

12.1. Forging a New Relationship with Your Ex . . . . . . . . . . . . . 36

12.2. Cultivating Your Single Parent Identity . . . . . . . . . . . . . . 37

12.3. Establishing a Co-Parenting Strategy . . . . . . . . . . . . . . . . 38

12.4. Finding Your Inner Strength . . . . . . . . . . . . . . . . . . . . . . 38

12.5. Carrying Onward: Building Your Future . . . . . . . . . . . . . . 39

# Chapter 1. Introduction

Embark on a heartfelt journey with the "Diverse Divorce: Parenting through Separation" special report. This treasure trove of insights bursts with strategies, personal stories, and expert perspectives to facilitate a smoother transition for families during challenging times of separation. You'll encounter stories of resilience and practical advice that will empower you to persevere, assuring your bonds with your children remain strong despite the changes. Divorce might be a twist in your life narrative, but it doesn't have to be an unhappy ending for your family. By the close of this report, you'll be geared up with the knowledge and confidence to be the best parent you can be, even amidst the storm. So, why wait? Grab this special report and let's usher in a new perspective of understanding, compassion, and heartfelt parenting through the journey of separation.

# Chapter 2. Understanding the Journey of Separation

The journey through separation and divorce is a challenging one, testing even the most resilient of us. It's like traversing a labyrinth, with its twists and turns, not knowing which path will lead you to your destination. But with courage, understanding, open communication, and the right support, you can navigate this journey and ensure the welfare of your children whilst maintaining a healthy relationship with you ex-spouse.

## 2.1. Understanding Divorce

High among the truths universally acknowledged must be the fact that divorce is tough. It is a seismic event that shakes the very foundation of your life - personally, socially, financially, and emotionally. It is more than just the dissolution of a marriage; it is the unraveling of a shared life and the dreams that came with it.

However, coming to grips with the end of a marital relationship is the first, crucial step toward rebuilding your life and helping your children adjust. Being well-informed about the emotional stages of divorce can be incredibly helpful here. They may be similar to the stages of grief, moving through denial, anger, bargaining, depression, and finally acceptance. Each person processes these stages differently, and the length of time spent on each stage varies.

## 2.2. Role of Communication

During divorce, open and honest communication is necessary both between the parents and the child and between the separated spouses. With children, the goal should be to reassure them that they are loved, and that their needs will continue to be met, so they maintain their sense of security.

With the other parent, strive to ensure discussions remain child-focused. Avoid using children as messengers or bargaining chips. Creating a communication plan can be beneficial, outlining when and how discussions and updates will take place. Clear, open, and respectful communication is key.

# 2.3. Coping Strategies

As you navigate the journey of separating, you need to prioritize healthy coping mechanisms for both yourself and your children. These might include seeking professional help like counselling, self-care activities, turning to support networks like friends and family, or joining support groups. It's vital not to allow pain and turmoil to cloud your behavior and responses.

Maintaining routine can be a potent coping strategy, particularly for children. It provides a comforting sense of order and predictability amidst the turbulence of divorce.

# 2.4. Co-Parenting

The separation of spouses does not entail the termination of parental roles. A vital part of the journey of separation is learning how to co-parent effectively, despite the relationships between you as a couple changing.

Establishing a co-parenting agreement that outlines rules, visitation rights, education, healthcare, and financial arrangements is a start. The focus should always be on what is best for the child. On-going communication about the children's progress, challenges, and any changes in routines or behavior should be maintained.

## 2.5. Building Resilience

Resilience is the key to recovering from and successfully adjusting to changes in life. It's about learning from past experiences, bouncing back from setbacks, and continuing to move forward.

Both parents and children will need to build resilience during the divorce process. For parents, this could mean self-care activities, therapy, mindfulness-based stress reduction practices, or seeking support from friends and family. For children, parents can help them build resilience by being sensitive to their needs, providing a stable and supportive environment, and encouraging open discussions about their feelings.

## 2.6. Final Thoughts

Understanding the journey of separation involves recognizing the various stages, acknowledging your emotions, and taking requisite steps to cope with the changes. Implementing effective communication strategies, co-parenting effectively, and fostering a resilient mindset in yourself and your children are integral parts of this journey.

Although this path is strenuous, with patience, understanding, perseverance, and support, you can successfully navigate your way, ensuring your bonds with your children remain strong. You are not alone, and remember, there is always a possibility of brighter days ahead, unfolding a new chapter of understanding, compassion, and heartfelt parenting.

# Chapter 3. Priorities in Parenting through Change

The reality of parenting is that the process is dynamic, constantly adapting and responding to a variety of factors, including changes in family structure. Change in the form of familial separation or divorce can dramatically impact the priority areas in your parenting approach.

## 3.1. Change: Understanding and Navigating Through It

Change—no matter what form it takes—can be a challenging and often emotional venture. The impact of familial transition, especially separation or divorce, can significantly disrupt the norm, leading to a ripple effect across all aspects of life. Understanding change, and learning to navigate through it effectively, is crucial to making the transition smoother for everyone involved.

Firstly, understand that change is a process. It doesn't happen overnight. There will be stages, each with its challenges and triumphs. Knowing this will aid you in cultivating patience and resilience—a core strength that will benefit you and your children as you navigate the changes ahead.

Secondly, remember the importance of communication. Essentially, clarity breeds understanding and reduces the potential for misunderstanding. Parents should communicate about the changes directly with their children, addressing concerns and answering questions truthfully while considerate of their ages and maturity levels. Through communication, you can make sure your child feels heard and understood during this era of change.

# 3.2. Recognizing the Needs of Your Child

Parenting requires responsiveness to your child's needs, and this might be more crucial than ever during times of separation or divorce. Through all the adjustments, upheavals, and modifications, your child's core needs—security, love, self-esteem, and others—remain consistent.

Your top priority should always be meeting these needs. Modifying your existence routine, making your child feel loved and cherished, ensuring their self-esteem is nurtured—these are indispensable determinants in helping your child weather the storm.

Understanding your child's requirements will help you mount a powerful response to these needs. This could involve maintaining consistency in routines to create a sense of stability, spending quality time even with time constraints, or encouraging expression of feelings, among other strategies.

# 3.3. Healthy Coping Mechanisms

In times of change, encouraging healthy coping mechanisms can greatly mitigate the potential negative impacts on your child's emotional health. They will feel anxious, scared, and perhaps betrayed due to the changes happening around them.

Promote outlets for expression and emotional venting such as artistic activities, journaling, or sports. Encourage your child to maintain friendships and social connections which can provide a sense of continuity. It may be beneficial to seek external professional support if required.

Above all, make sure to exemplify healthy coping yourself. You are your child's role model. They learn how to deal with stress, changes, and difficulties by observing how you manage them.

## 3.4. Co-Parenting Successfully

Co-parenting can come with its challenges, but it also offers an opportunity to provide a stable and loving environment for your children post-separation. It's always the best scenario when both parents can be involved and supportive for the sake of their children.

Strive to maintain open and honest communication with your co-parent. Keep your children out of any conflicts or disagreements. Cooperate and make decisions keeping your child's best interests in mind. Be respectful of each other's time and maintain consistent routines for your child across both households.

Invest in co-parenting apps or tools if necessary, to schedule and track child-related obligations and to ensure smoother communication.

## 3.5. The Role of Self-Care in Parenting

Don't overlook your needs in the process. Remember that well-being is contagious. If you are well-cared for and content, your child is likely to mirror this positive state. Implement a self-care routine incorporating physical, mental, and emotional wellness strategies.

Regular exercise, a balanced diet, and adequate sleep form the foundation of physical self-care. Emotional well-being can be managed through regular timeouts, mindfulness activities, hobbies, or seeking support from friends, family, or professionals when required.

Navigating change might be challenging, but remember it can be managed and even turned into an opportunity, a meaningful period of growth for you and your children. Be patient, responsive, and loving, and you can undoubtedly lead your family through the storm.

# Chapter 4. Communicating Divorce to Children: Paths Less Travelled

Communicating the news of a divorce to children can seem like a daunting task. It is, after all, a delicate process, one that necessitates the highest degree of understanding and compassion. However, by adopting some less traveled yet effective paths, this conversation can transpire more smoothly. Through a blend of expert advice, personal stories from parents, and enlightened strategies, you can learn to traverse this complex terrain with confidence and grace.

## 4.1. Comfort Comes First

Before diving into the realm of divorce talks, it's essential to ensure that your children feel loved and secure. Communicating in a comforting and secure environment, such as your family room, can have a substantial impact on how your children receive the news. Perhaps you could seat them on the couch, cushions and all, where many a bedtime story has been shared and giggles have echoed. Giving due consideration to the timing is crucial too. Choose a moment when there's no rush - no looming sports practice or school the next day. This calm envelop can significantly influence their emotional states during, and subsequent to, the discussion.

## 4.2. Rehearse to De-Stress

Practicing what to say can have a considerable impact on your ability to deliver the news to your children lucidly and persuasively. It can help parents avoid becoming overly emotional or resorting to blame. From choosing the right words to deciding the order of the information - rehearse, revise, and ready yourself. Practice with a friend or a therapist to get feedback and support. You might even consider recording your practice sessions, so you can evaluate your tone and expressions. Observing your own reactions can help you modulate your emotions better when you confront the real situation.

# 4.3. Simple, Straightforward, and Age-Appropriate Talk

When you finally sit down with your children, it's crucial to deliver the news in the simplest, clearest manner possible. Depending on their ages, your children may not fully grasp the concept of divorce. Younger children, for example, don't need detailed explanations about why the separation is happening, just that Mom and Dad won't be living together anymore. Simultaneously, adolescents and teenagers might seek more information about the changes that will ensue. Remember always to talk in terms they can comprehend.

# 4.4. The United Front

Presenting the decision as a unified front can be beneficial in ensuring that your children know the decision was mutual. This can go a long way in avoiding any feelings of guilt or blame your child might feel. Using phrases such as 'we have decided' or 'both of us think' can reinforce this notion of unity in decision-making.

# 4.5. Reassurance - The Power of Love

The primary question looming in your children's minds during this conversation will likely be: Mom and Dad are separating, does this mean they'll stop loving me too? Reinforce the fact that your love for them is ceaseless, unconditional, and independent of your marital status. Children need reassurance, both through words and deeds, that they indeed are loved.

# 4.6. Addressing the Changes

While you needn't go into all future arrangements' specifics during the initial conversation, your children will need to understand how their day-to-day lives will change. Explain the new living arrangements and how this might affect their school, sports, or other activities. Keep the conversation as neutral and positive as possible.

# 4.7. Checking-In

Checking in with your children after the initial conversation is vital. It allows for their anxieties or queries to be addressed timely. Regular check-ins can also help you gauge their coping levels while reminding them that you're there to guide them through this challenging period.

While each divorce experience is unique, these guidelines provide an overall strategy to help you communicate this life-altering news to your children. Remember, it's a journey not just for you, but for your children as well. Your efforts to share, communicate, and reassure will go a long way in helping them navigate their emotions successfully, aiding them in the long run.

# Chapter 5. The Art of Co-Parenting Post-Separation

As you find yourself in the throes of separation, co-parenting can initially seem like a daunting task. With a myriad of emotions at play, the ultimate focus should remain on providing a nurturing environment for your children. Embracing the art of co-parenting can help ensure your children feel loved, secure, and resilient during this challenging time.

## 5.1. Establishing Clear and Consistent Communication

Clear communication between co-parents is essential. Open and regular dialogue will help prevent misunderstandings and ensure both parents are on common ground regarding the children's care. The format can be a simple weekly phone call or email exchange. Do not let personal disagreements cloud the essential topic: the well-being of your children.

Be aware of your tone during these exchanges. Strive for kindness, respect, and patience. Understand that your ex-partner is making equal sacrifices and adjustments for co-parenting to work. Respect their difficulties too.

## 5.2. Developing a Co-Parenting Plan

A well-defined plan can greatly ease out the co-parenting processes. The plan should ideally cover details about which parent will host the children and when, how you'll handle holidays and special events, scheduled times for communication about the children's needs, and how you'll tackle inevitable future conflicts.

Step back from personal feelings of disappointment or anger, and think in terms of practicalities, fairness, and comfort for your children. Over time, you might need to make changes to the plan as children's needs evolve.

## 5.3. Fostering Emotional Stability for the Children

Keep your children shielded from the emotional turmoil of your separation. Constant exposure to conflict and negative emotions can impair their emotional growth. Foster a home environment that exudes love, care, and positivity.

Let your children express their feelings without fear of judgment. Encourage them to communicate openly about their worries and reassure them with comfort and guidance. It's perfectly alright for them to love both parents and miss the one they aren't currently with.

## 5.4. Creating and Maintaining Boundaries

Drawing firm boundaries helps avoid unnecessary conflict and confusion. The most effective co-parenting occurs when both parties respect each other's personal space, parenting time, and roles and responsibilities.

Healthy boundaries also apply to your communication. Discuss things directly with your co-parent instead of passing messages through your children. This shields them from potential tension and conflict.

Respect your co-parent's time with the children. Don't plan activities that might infringe on their time, involve yourself in their activities, or invade their home unless invited or in case of emergencies.

## 5.5. Cultivating Patience and Understanding

Patience and understanding are key pillars to guard yourself and your children from the rocky waves of emotions. Separation doesn't just impact you and your ex-partner; it's a time of change for everyone involved, including your children.

Challenging situations will arise, even if you have well-laid plans. An exercise in patience and understanding is vital in those moments. Allow room for errors, forgive, and focus on solutions rather than dwell on the problems.

## 5.6. Emphasizing Teamwork and Flexibility

At the heart of successful co-parenting lies a strong sense of teamwork. Acting as a cohesive unit assures your children of your undying love and support, despite the circumstances.

Unexpected changes are a part of life that you need to incorporate into your co-parenting journey. Be cooperative and accommodating where possible, especially when it is to the benefit of your children. With time, a certain rhythm will fall into place that becomes second nature.

Throughout this journey, remember the ultimate goal: to raise happy, confident, and well-adjusted children. Co-parenting can be complex, but by implementing these strategies, fostering open communication, and focusing on your children's needs above your own emotional discomforts, you'll be one step closer to mastering the art of co-parenting.

# Chapter 6. Navigating Child Emotions: Tears and Cheers

Divorce is a challenging moment, not just for the parents involved, but also for the children who are often caught in the whirlwind of the situation. As parents, it's crucial to understand that your child may experience a range of emotions that can be challenging to navigate. During this time, emotions like sadness, anger, confusion, and relief may coexist.

## 6.1. Recognizing the Tears: Understanding Your Child's Emotional Response to Divorce

Every child reacts differently to their parents' divorce, and understanding this response is the first step toward helping them through this difficult period. This requires a deep awareness of the emotional terrain your child is traversing.

Children may respond immediately with strong emotions or may react much later. Some children may express sadness or grief, while others may exhibit anger, fear, or even denial about the situation. Many times, younger children believe that they are somehow responsible for their parents' separation. Dealing with each of these emotions necessitates different strategies.

## 6.2. Addressing Anger and Frustration

It's not uncommon for a child to display anger or frustration during a divorce. They may feel powerless and may express this through raised voices, tantrums, or even violent behavior.

To address this, there are a few key steps:

1. Always keep an open line of communication with your child. Let them express their frustration and validate their feeling of anger without encouraging harmful behavior.

2. Set clear boundaries and explain the consequences for unacceptable behavior. Make them understand that feeling angry is normal, but aggression towards others is not acceptable.

3. Lastly, help your child find healthy outlets for their anger. This may include physical exercise, creative outlets like drawing or writing, or even counselling sessions.

# 6.3. Managing Fear

Fear is another common emotion expressed by children going through parents' divorce. This fear can stem from uncertainty about the future, fear of losing a parent, or anxiety about changes in living arrangements.

To help manage your child's fear:

1. Give your child as much information as possible about the upcoming changes. Let them know what will happen next and reassure them that both parents will continue to love and care for them.

2. Maintain routines as much as possible to give your child a sense of stability.

3. Encourage open conversations about their feelings and fears. Make it safe for them to share their concerns with you.

# 6.4. Dealing with Sadness and Grief

Feeling sad or experiencing grief is a natural response for children to their parents' divorce. Here's how you can support them during this phase:

1. Be patient and allow them to go through the grieving process.

2. Comfort them, reminding that it's perfectly okay to feel sad and that both parents are there for them despite the separation.

3. Encourage them to express their sadness, whether it's through talking, drawing, or other forms of expression.

4. Consider seeking the help of a professional counselor or therapist, especially if the feelings of sadness persist or worsen.

# 6.5. Tackling Guilt and Denial

Children often struggle with guilt, believing that they have caused the divorce, while others may go into denial, convincing themselves that the separation is temporary.

Help them understand and navigate these feelings by:

1. Reassuring them that the divorce is not their fault.

2. Being honest about the permanence of the situation without being harsh, preparing them for the new reality of their family structure.

# 6.6. Cultivating the Cheers: Building Resilience and Positivity Amidst Divorce

While handling the negative emotions is important, it's equally crucial to foster a positive and resilient mindset in your child during a divorce. Children possess an inherent ability to adapt, and with careful guidance, they can navigate this difficult time with much more ease than you might anticipate.

## 6.7. Resilience-Building Games and Activities

Resilience-building activities can be a fun and effective way to help children handle their emotions. Activities may include collaborative games that promote teamwork, interactive stories about dealing with change, or resilience-themed arts and crafts. Always follow up these activities with open-ended questions that allow the child to reflect on what they've learned and how they can apply it to their situation.

## 6.8. Coping Strategies

Encourage coping strategies such as deep breathing, meditation, or yoga to help manage stress. Teach them about 'feeling words' to express their emotions more understandably. Model positive behavior yourself and show them how you cope with change in a positive and healthy manner.

## 6.9. Rebuilding Trust

Trust can often become strained during a divorce, especially if it was conflict-laden. It's crucial to rebuild your child's trust during this time:

1. Keep promises to show that even though circumstances have changed, your reliability hasn't.

2. Be honest- let them know about changes beforehand, and admit if things are tough. At their level of understanding, explain why

decisions were made.

3. Regularly remind them that both parents cherish and love them.

Remember, effective navigation through these emotional waters can have lasting positive impacts. It not only addresses the immediate situation at hand but also equips your child with coping skills that can benefit them throughout their life.

# Chapter 7. Legal Landscapes: Children's Rights and Custody

A profound understanding of the legal sphere regarding children's rights and custody plays a pivotal role in your navigation through this challenging phase of your family life.

## 7.1. Understanding Children's Rights

Children, as a demographic sector, possess separate rights, meant to ensure their protection and welfare, including the right to express their opinion, the right to love and be loved, and, most importantly in the context of divorce, the right to a secure and stable family environment.

One vital aspect of children's rights is that their rights do not cease to exist with the rupture of their parents' union. The United Nations Convention on the Rights of the Child (UNCRC), the most accepted international agreement on children's rights, asserts a child's principal right to grow in a cohesive family setting.

In circumstances where the family unit dissolves, various local, regional, and national entities are committed to ascertaining that the child's rights are upheld, notably the right to maintain regular touch with both parents unless it's contrary to the child's best interests.

# 7.2. Unravelling the Concept of Custody

The term 'custody' carries various meanings that can sometimes lead to misunderstandings. However, it principally refers to the legal duty and authority that a parent has over a child, as recognized by the law. It primarily covers two key aspects: decision-making rights (legal custody) and dwelling rights (physical custody). Every court puts the child's welfare before any other considerations when determining custody arrangements.

The dissolution of a marriage doesn't annul parental responsibilities. Both parents are usually obligated to continue providing for their child's material, emotional, and educational needs. This constitutional provision remains, whether or not the spouses decide to lead separate lives.

Physical custody refers to which parent the child will live with—the one who wins this arrangement enjoys the moral and legal right to live with the child. The noncustodial parent is usually granted visitation rights (unless it's deemed harmful), ensuring they continue playing a parental role.

Legal custody, on the other hand, determines who makes major decisions regarding the child's life. These could include choices about education, health, religious matters, and native language, among others.

# 7.3. Common Custody Arrangements

Several custody arrangements are prevalent in modern society; primary among these are sole and joint custody.

Sole custody, as the name suggests, grants one parent both physical and legal custody. The noncustodial parent's role, in this case, is limited to visitation and is excluded from decision-making aspects.

Joint custody, alternatively, allows both parents to carry on their parental duties in full capacity, irrespective of their interpersonal relationship. Joint legal custody ensures each parent's say in major decisions about their child's life, whereas joint physical custody allows the child to divide their time between both parents.

# 7.4. The Role of the Courts in Custody Decisions

The court assumes a crucial role in dictating custody rights and each parent's role. Its goal is safeguarding the minor child's best interests. This involves considering various factors, such as the child's age, mental and physical health of parents, child's relationship with each parent, each parent's capacity to provide for the child, stability of home environment, and, at times, the child's own wishes.

Although traditionally, mothers tended to win custody over their minor children, gender roles have shifted significantly. Nowadays, courts assess the actual parenting capacities rather than relying on gender-stereotypical roles.

Despite the legal intricacies involved, understanding the above concepts will bring a sense of clarity to your unique situation. Remember, the journey through a divorce can be challenging, but when the focus remains on the welfare of your child and respecting their rights, it can create a conduit for a healthier transition for everyone involved.

# 7.5. Legal Representation for Children

To alleviate the potential impact of parental disagreement on children during custody disputes, some jurisdictions have begun to adopt legal representation for children. This is typically either a guardian ad litem or a children's lawyer, both of whom are tasked with representing the interests of children in court. While they serve the same general purpose, there are subtle differences in role and methodology between the two.

Knowing the ins and outs of the laws that pertain to children's rights and parental duties—like custody— can make the divorce process less daunting and more manageable, ensuring a potentially smoother transition for your family. Arm yourself with knowledge, understanding, and patience. As you reconfigure your life post-divorce, remember that it's an opportunity, not an endpoint.

Understanding these parameters will contribute to a more fluent, efficient process that prioritizes the emotional well-being and rights of your child. Keep abreast of the legal landscapes so that your parenting journey may be one marked by strength, mindfulness, and compassion in the face of separation. The navigation may be complex, but knowing the terrain always makes a journey smoother.

# Chapter 8. Alone, not Lonely: Redefining Solo Parenting

In the midst of separation or divorce, you may find yourself transitioning from co-parenting to solo parenting. This phase of life can be challenging but also offers an opportunity to redefine your role and your relationship with your children. Through a strategic blend of resilience, patience, love, and a different perspective, you can turn this seeming difficulty into an open avenue for stronger bonds.

## 8.1. Reigniting Your Personal Identity

Transitioning to solo parenting also means reshuffling your personal deck. You're not just a parent; you're also an individual with your own identity. Refinding yourself can not only foster personal growth but also empower you to bring your best-self into the parenting sphere. Don't forget to set time aside for self-reflection and self-care. Do the things that you love and that make you feel confident and self-assured. Remember, a happier and healthier you directly impact the happiness and health of your children.

## 8.2. Building a Strong Support Network

Surviving a changing tide of family dynamics requires a strong support system around you. You don't have to do everything alone. Start by reaching out to friends and family who genuinely care about you and your journey. Also seek professional help such as therapists, lawyers, or professional caregivers, if necessary. Engage with local community groups or online forums to form a network of parents experiencing similar transitions. These interactions often provide a treasure trove of practical advice and emotional support.

## 8.3. Strengthening Communication Channels

Effective communication plays a pivotal role in solo parenting. Be open and honest with your children about the changes they're experiencing, taking into account their age and understanding. Establish regular check-ins with your children to gauge their emotional temperature amidst the changes. Always reaffirm your love for them and reinforce that the separation is in no way their fault.

## 8.4. Fine-tuning Parenting Strategies

As a solo parent, tweaking your parenting strategies is essential. You're now the captain of the ship; you'll need to distribute tasks and chores around your household more evenly, without shifting all responsibility on your children. Innovate new family traditions and routines to provide a sense of consistency and security. Empower your children with a level of age-appropriate responsibility and independence but be sure to provide support whenever they need it.

## 8.5. Nurturing Emotional Resilience

Your emotional resilience greatly influences your children. It's normal to have a blend of emotions, but it's essential to manage these in a healthy manner. Utilize stress management techniques like deep breathing, meditation, or regular physical activity. Articulate your feelings to a trusted confidante. Also, assure your children it's natural to feel a mix of emotions and encourage them to express their feelings openly, too.

## 8.6. Quality Time and Unwavering Love

Love is the irreplaceable cornerstone in parenting. Your love for your children provides them the security they need in this tumultuous phase. Set aside quality time for your children, individually or collectively, making sure they always feel cherished. Create a nurturing and understanding environment for your children where they feel comfortable confiding in you.

## 8.7. Building Financial Stability

A part of solo parenting includes shouldering the financial responsibilities. It's critical to plan out a financial structure that can accommodate your lifestyle as a solo parent. Whether it's budgeting, saving, or investing, ensure you have a secure financial plan that can sustain your family through thick and thin.

Being a solo parent can feel like a tightrope walk, but remember, you're capable and stronger than you think. Use every challenge as an opportunity to grow and develop robust bonds with your children. Lastly, realize it's okay to seek help and it's okay to take time for yourself. You're not just a parent moving through a separation or divorce; you're a resilient person paving a path for a stronger, more loving relationship with your children.

# Chapter 9. Resilience: Thriving in the Face of Challenge

Resilience doesn't happen in a vacuum; it is cultivated through experiences, both pleasant and challenging, that empower us to thrive even in the most difficult circumstances.

## 9.1. Understanding Resilience

Resilience is our ability to adapt and recover from adversities. It's our capacity to bounce back from difficult experiences and stresses in life, from minor issues like a dispute with a spouse, to major life-changing events like divorce, or job loss. More importantly, resilience is not just about surviving adversities but also about thriving despite them, and sometimes because of them.

Everyone has resilience—it's just a matter of how much and how well it's utilized. A key aspect of resilience is emotional intelligence, which involves recognizing, understanding, and managing our own and others' emotions. Those who exhibit emotional intelligence tend to display higher levels of resilience because of their ability to remain calm under stress, empathize with others, and communicate effectively.

## 9.2. Building Resilience

Building resilience is a dynamic process that requires time and patience. It's not about avoiding obstacles or jumping a certain hurdle with ease. Instead, it is about confronting challenges head-on and making the most of what we learn in the process.

There are numerous strategies that can enhance your resilience:

1. Continually developing emotional intelligence: Enhance your self-awareness, learn to manage your emotions, improve your self-motivation, develop empathy, and hone social skills.

2. Maintaining a positive outlook: A positive attitude helps handle stress more effectively.

3. Taking care of your physical health: Regular exercise, balanced diet, adequate sleep—these core health principles remain untouched when it comes to nurturing resilience.

4. Nurturing a resilient mindset: Life is full of ups and downs; fostering a flexible and open mindset can help navigate these twists and turns.

# 9.3. Resilience and Separation

When it comes to separation or divorce, resilience becomes even more crucial. Divorce is seldom easy; it involves a major disruption in the family structure which can be stressful for all parties involved. Yet, it is through these challenging times that we have the opportunity to foster our resilience.

Firstly, understanding that it's okay to feel upset, angry, or frightened during a divorce is crucial. It's essential not just to feel these emotions but also to express them in a healthy manner. Bottling up emotions can lead to high-stress levels, while outbursts can impact relationships negatively.

Next, adopting a solution-oriented approach can help. Instead of dwelling on the problem, focus on figuring out ways to resolve it. Foster an accepting mindset—accept that the situation has occurred, learn from it, and move forward.

# 9.4. A Model of Resilience

There is no one-size-fits-all model of resilience, but that doesn't mean we don't have guides to follow. At its core, resilience relies on four key components: awareness, adaptability, confidence, and hope.

- Awareness: Reflect upon your situation and acknowledge your emotions. Understand what triggered certain reactions and use that knowledge to respond rather than react to future situations.

- Adaptability: Embrace change instead of resisting it. See change as an opportunity to explore new things and get to know different facets of yourself.

- Confidence: Believe in your ability to handle any situation that comes your way. Draw upon past experiences where you overcame hardship.

- Hope: Maintain a hopeful and optimistic outlook even in the face of adversity.

Divorce is difficult, but by building resilience, it can become an opportunity to grow, a chance to redefine yourself and relationships with others. With resilience, we can navigate the challenges of separation, handle the stressful days, and move forward with understanding and compassion.

# 9.5. Setting an Example

For parents, your resilience during this tense and emotional divorce period also serves as a model for your children. By displaying emotional strength, maintaining a positive outlook, and dealing sensitively with the situation, you can demonstrate to your children how to handle crises.

Children are perceptive; they take cues from the adults around them. Seeing their parents tackle hardships with resilience will instill in them the strength and the capacity to cope with their own challenges, both now and in the future. An empathetic, patient, and composed demeanor will make them feel secure and loved, despite the changes happening in their lives.

We wish resilience was an inherent capability we could tap into at will, but it's not. It needs cultivation through supportive relationships, nurturing a positive view of oneself and accepting change as a part of living. Remember, it's not about bouncing back to the same old person you were before the crisis hit, it's about growing through the crisis and emerging stronger, more compassionate, and wiser. Resilience doesn't mean the pain doesn't affect you; it just means you keep going despite the pain. And in the process, you show your children how to do the same.

# Chapter 10. Healing Together: Empathetic Parent-Child approaches

The initial impulse, when faced with the effects of divorce on children, is often to shield them from the pain or to hide our own distress from them. However, it's essential to acknowledge that, like you, your child is navigating the choppy waters of the separation. Embracing a more empathetic perspective can make the journey less intimidating for both of you, fostering not just surviving but healing and thriving in this new turn in your lives.

## 10.1. Navigating Conversations about Divorce

When it comes to discussing the subject of divorce, it's important to keep lines of communication open. This can be challenging when yourself you're learning to cope with these new circumstances. Providing an age-appropriate explanation about the situation allows the child to understand the changes happening in a more secure way.

- Address their Inquiries: Always be ready to answer your child's questions. They might be simple like 'why is dad/mom not at home?' or more complex ones like 'Did I cause your divorce?' It's essential to reassure the child that the separation was not their fault.

- Honesty is Vital: Children are highly observant. While it's crucial to share age-appropriate information, honesty remains paramount. Use appropriate language to explain the situation, but ensure not to overshare details that might cause additional distress.

- Listen to their Feelings: Allow your child to express themselves openly. It normalizes their feelings and validates their thoughts, helping them feel more assured.

# 10.2. The Art of Active Listening

Active listening is a complementary skill to effective communication. It involves fully focusing on, understanding, responding, and then remembering what's being said.

- Show Genuine Interest: Ask open-ended questions that allow your child to articulate their thoughts and feelings freely. Nod, maintain eye contact, and use small verbal comments like 'uh-huh' to show you are paying attention.

- Encourage with Care: Use phrases like 'I see,' 'Tell me more about...' or 'Could you explain a little more about...,' to encourage your child to share more.

- Reflect, Interpret and Clarify: Paraphrase what your child has told you to ensure you've understood them correctly. If any confusion arises, don't hesitate to ask for clarification.

# 10.3. Sharing Feelings: Creating a Safe Space

Creating a safe emotional space for your child to express their feelings is integral in nurturing resilience and strengthening your bond. It may also help your child make sense of their turbulent emotions.

- Encourage Emotional Expression: Teach your child that it's okay to feel certain feelings. Practice identifying and naming emotions together. Consider tools such as feeling charts or emotional health books for children.

- Practice Emotional Validation: Practice phrases like, 'I can understand why you're feeling that way,' or, 'Your feelings are valid,' to help establish an environment where your child feels understood and validated.

- Emotional Cohesion: Be keen to spend quality time together. Dedicating portions of your time to enjoy shared activities can cultivate mutual understanding and bonding, providing emotional stability for your child throughout this challenging period.

# 10.4. Tools for Transition: Managing Change Together

Utilize various tools to help your child cope with the transitions that come with divorce.

- Routines Matter: Familiar routines give a child the comfort of predictability amidst change. Try keeping bedtime, meals, and other daily routines intact.

- Visual Reassurances: Use calendars or timelines to visually represent the changes that will occur and when.

- Child-Centric Time: Avoid the parental tug-of-war. Be sure to focus on your child's needs when scheduling visitation or managing new living arrangements.

# 10.5. Co-Parenting: The Power of Collaboration

Co-parenting can be challenging in the aftermath of separation. Yet, prioritizing co-operation and flexibility can alleviate your child's pain during the transition period.

- Consistent Messaging: Strive to maintain a united front when addressing your child's concerns about the divorce. This consistency reinforces feelings of security.

- Co-Parenting Tools: Consider using tools and apps designed for divorced parents to aid communication, manage schedules, and share important child-related information.

- Respect and Cooperation: The level of respect between separated parents can greatly influence a child's transition. Avoid putting your child in the middle of any conflicts.

# Chapter 11. Resilience in Action: Building Your Child's Strength

Resilience is not a trait that people either have or do not have. It involves behaviours, thoughts, and actions that can be learned and developed.

- Encourage Problem-Solving: Help your child identify potential solutions to problems, weigh pros and cons, and choose an appropriate response.

- Practice Optimism: Teach your child to see the optimistic side of situations without dismissing valid feelings of sadness or frustration.

- Understand Impermanence: Teach your child that feelings and situations, including this challenging one, are temporary. This can foster hope as they grapple with changes.

As parents navigate the rocky terrains of divorce, remembering to integrate empathy and open communication into your parenting approach can pave the way for a smoother transition. Give your child space, validate their feelings, encourage their expression, and most importantly, assure them of your unfaltering love and support. Separation can be a tough phase, but together, you can transform it into a journey of understanding, healing, and growth.

# Chapter 12. New Beginnings: Building Life Post-Divorce

The ink is finally dry on your divorce decree. For weeks, months, or possibly even years, your life's been consumed with court dates, paperwork, and tensions. It's over now. You're standing atop a mountain of change, looking out at the strange, new landscape of your life post-divorce. Yet, amidst the uncertainty, there's an undeniable sensation, a shimmer of excitement, because a divorce, while undeniably an end, is also a beginning.

## 12.1. Forging a New Relationship with Your Ex

For the sake of your children and your sanity, you'll need to construct a new kind of relationship with your ex-spouse. This relationship takes many forms and evolves over time, but the beginnings are dictated by how you communicate.

1. Treat your ex-spouse as a business partner.

2. Choose your battles wisely.

3. Adopt a solution-oriented approach to conflicts.

Let's delve deeper into these points.

A business-like relationship with your ex-spouse might feel strange at first, but it creates an emotional buffer that prevents potential flare-ups and maintains focus on the well-being of the children. This approach allows you to set boundaries.

Choosing your battles wisely is pivotal in maintaining peace. Not every disagreement warrants a fight. There's virtue in learning when to stand your ground and when to let things slide.

Finally, adopting a solution-oriented attitude toward conflicts will be critically useful. Instead of pointing fingers during disagreements, shift the focus to finding a solution that is in the best interest of your children.

# 12.2. Cultivating Your Single Parent Identity

The transformation from being a part of a marital unit to becoming a single parent is a journey in itself. You have to redefine your identity in the context of your new situation. Here are some steps for establishing your single parent identity.

1. Recognize the shift in your reality.

2. Embrace the change.

3. Practice self-care.

Recognize your reality has changed. It's vital to accept your new role as a single parent. Though acceptance can be painful, it's essential for your emotional health and the health of your child.

Embracing change can seem intimidating. Once you're past the acceptance phase, it's necessary to embrace your new role as a single parent. See this change as an opportunity to grow and build a stronger bond with your child.

In the midst of all the change, remember to practice self-care. Taking care of your physical, mental, and emotional health isn't just vital for your well-being; it also sets an example for your children about the importance of personal self-care.

# 12.3. Establishing a Co-Parenting Strategy

Co-parenting demands a lot from both parents, but it's crucial for your children's well-being. Formulating a fair and balanced co-parenting strategy is paramount.

1. Set up a parenting plan.

2. Be prepared for different parenting styles.

3. Keep an open dialogue.

Setting up a parenting plan early in the post-divorce phase can alleviate future turmoil. This plan delineates the children's schedule, responsibility for school and extracurricular activities, and any other issues relating directly to the children.

Recognize that you and your ex might have different parenting styles, and that's ok. The important thing is to provide a loving, stable, and supportive environment for your children.

Keeping an open dialogue regarding co-parenting questions and concerns helps maintain the consistency vital for your children. Communication also helps in adjusting the parenting plan as your children grow and their needs change.

# 12.4. Finding Your Inner Strength

You will doubt your strength at times. It's ok. It's part of the process. But remember, you are stronger than you realize.

Watch the miracles that occur when life pushes you, and you push back. See the problem not as a crisis, but as a challenge, an opportunity. Forgive your slight stumbles, and celebrate your triumphs, no matter how small. Believe in yourself. You are embarking on the most challenging journey of resilience. You're building a life post-divorce, for your children, and most importantly, for yourself.

# 12.5. Carrying Onward: Building Your Future

Moving forward doesn't mean forgetting the past, but choosing to live fully in the present while planning for the future.

1. Start planning your financial future.

2. Create new family traditions.

3. Stay open to the possibility of love again.

The stability of your financial future is in your hands. Work on a financial plan, seek professional advice if needed. It might seem like a daunting task, but it will provide peace of mind in the long run.

Creating new family traditions with your children will help them adjust to the new family dynamics. These traditions will give them something to look forward to and remind them that even though the family dynamics have changed, the love and bond you share haven't.

Finally, stay open to the possibility of new love. It doesn't mean you have to start dating immediately. It simply means that you remain open to the possibility that love can find you again, at the right time.

Remember, life after divorce might be uncharted territory, but it's the beginning of a new chapter. It's the audacious start of a novel journey towards a future that's entirely yours to build.

www.ingramcontent.com/pod-product-compliance
Lightning Source LLC
Chambersburg PA
CBHW071612270726
48661CB00019B/3133